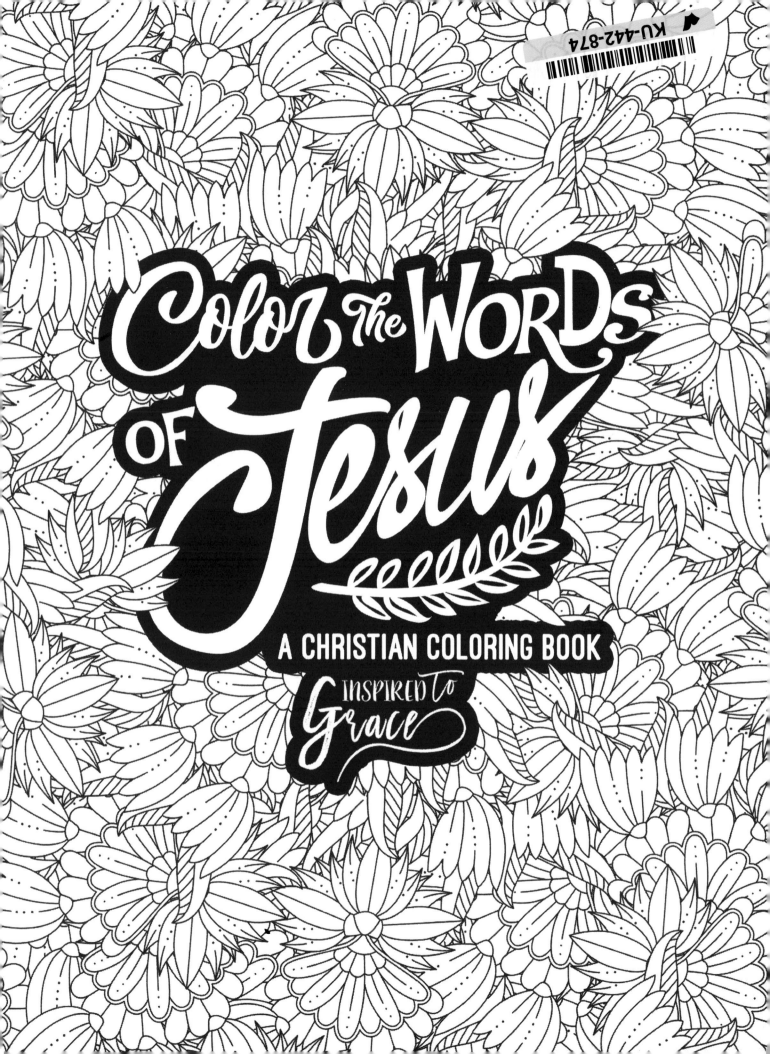

Color the WORDS OF Jesus

A CHRISTIAN COLORING BOOK

INSPIRED to GRACE

KU-442-874

Copyright © 2017 Inspired to Grace

Scripture quotations are from the following:

Scripture taken from the Holy Bible, NEW INTERNATIONAL VERSION®, NIV® Copyright © 1973, 1978, 1984, 2011 by Biblica, Inc.® Used by permission. All rights reserved worldwide. NEW INTERNATIONAL VERSION® and NIV® are registered trademarks of Biblica, Inc. Use of either trademark for the offering of goods or services requires the prior written consent of Biblica US, Inc.

Revised Standard Version of the Bible, copyright 1952 [2nd edition, 1971] by the Division of Christian Education of the National Council of the Churches of Christ in the United States of America. Used by permission. All rights reserved.

Scripture quotations marked HCSB®, are taken from the Holman Christian Standard Bible®, Copyright © 1999, 2000, 2002, 2003, 2009 by Holman Bible Publishers. Used by permission. HCSB® is a federally registered trademark of Holman Bible Publishers.

Scripture taken from the New King James Version. Copyright © 1982 by Thomas Nelson, Inc. Used by permission. All rights reserved.

The Holy Bible, King James Version. Cambridge Edition: 1769. Public Domain.

Scripture texts in this work are taken from the New American Bible, revised edition © 2010, 1991, 1986, 1970 Confraternity of Christian Doctrine, Washington, D.C. and are used by permission of the copyright owner. All Rights Reserved. No part of the New American Bible may be reproduced in any form without permission in writing from the copyright owner.

All rights reserved.

FREE DOWNLOAD

www.inspiredtograce.com/jesus

YOUR DOWNLOAD CODE: J3972

 @inspiredtograce

 Inspired to Grace

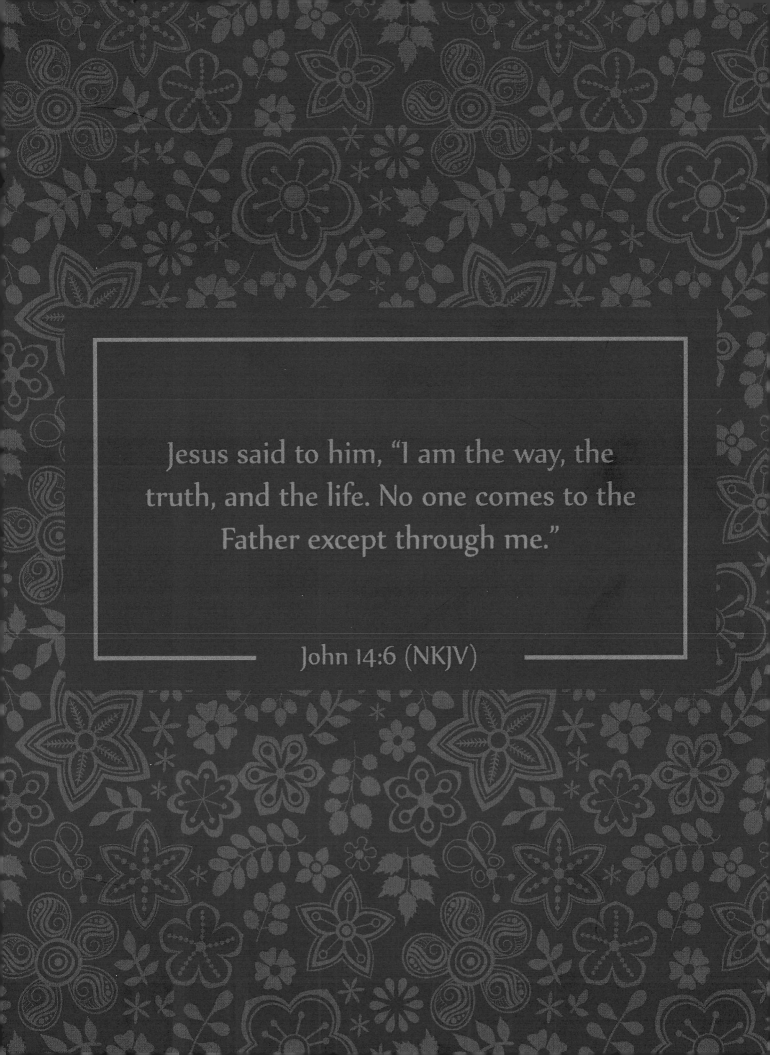

Jesus said to him, "I am the way, the truth, and the life. No one comes to the Father except through me."

John 14:6 (NKJV)

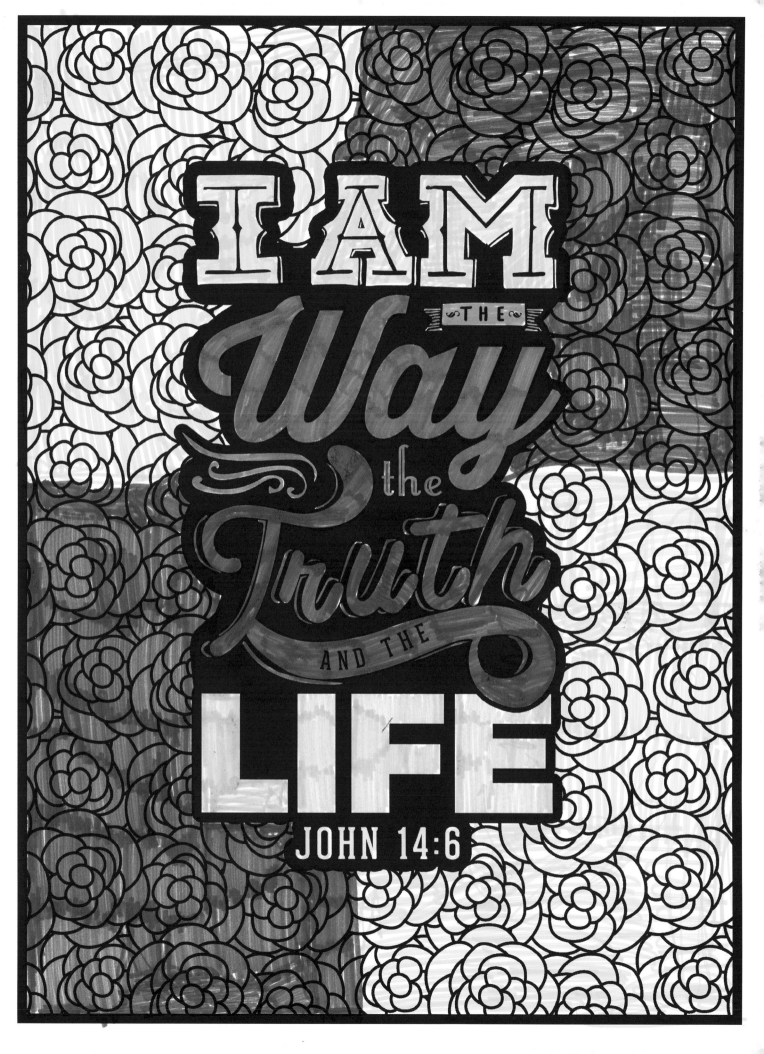

Jesus said to her, "I am the resurrection and the life. He who believes in me, though he may die, he shall live. And whoever lives and believes in me shall never die. Do you believe this?"

John 11:25-26 (NKJV)

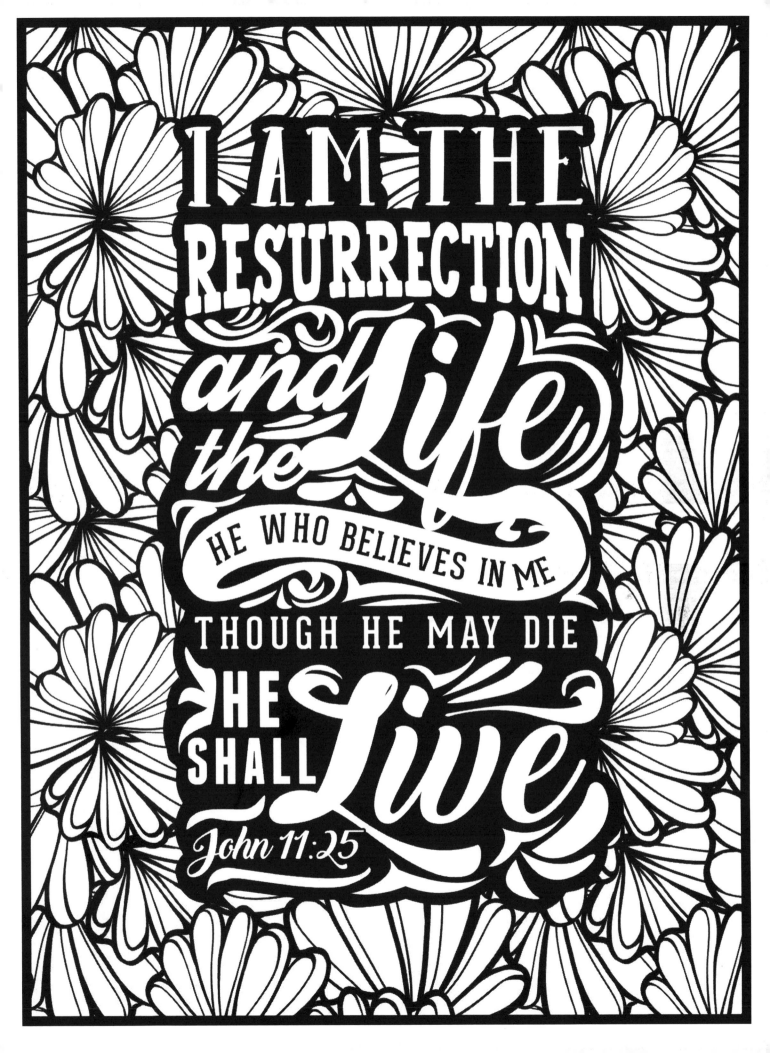

Jesus replied, "I am the bread of life. Whoever comes to me will never be hungry again. Whoever believes in me will never be thirsty."

John 6:35 (NLT)

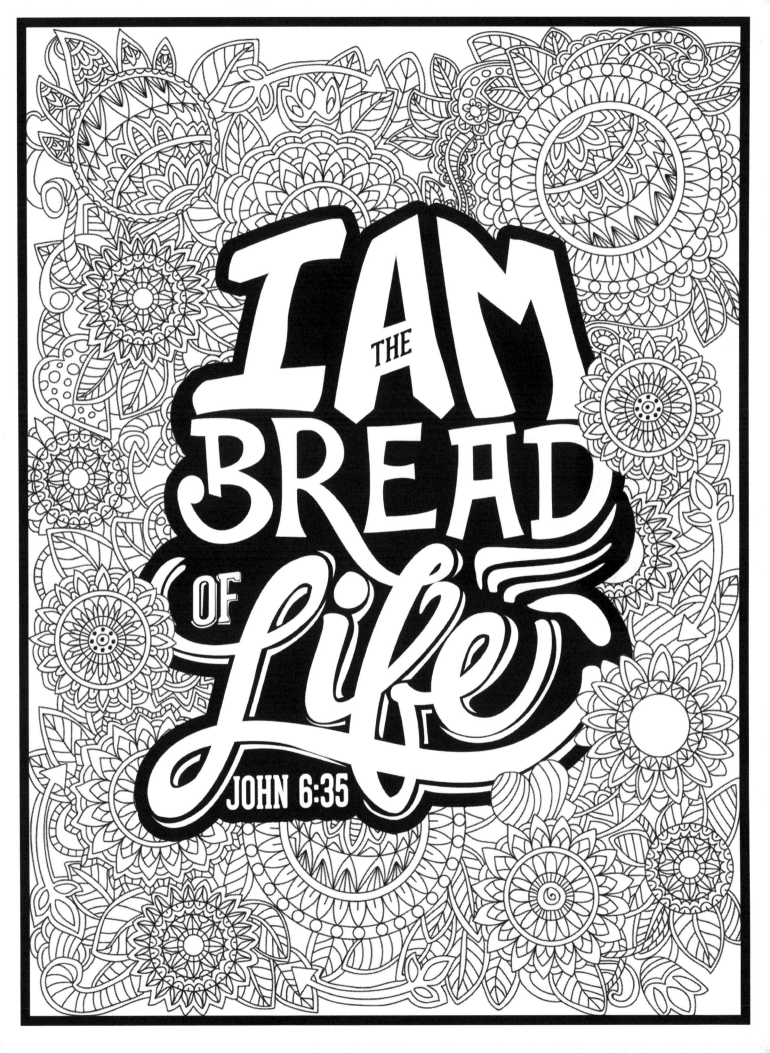

He said to him, "'You shall love the Lord your God with all your heart, and with all your soul, and with all your mind.' This is the greatest and first commandment. And a second is like it: 'You shall love your neighbor as yourself.'"

Matthew 22:37-39 (NRSV)

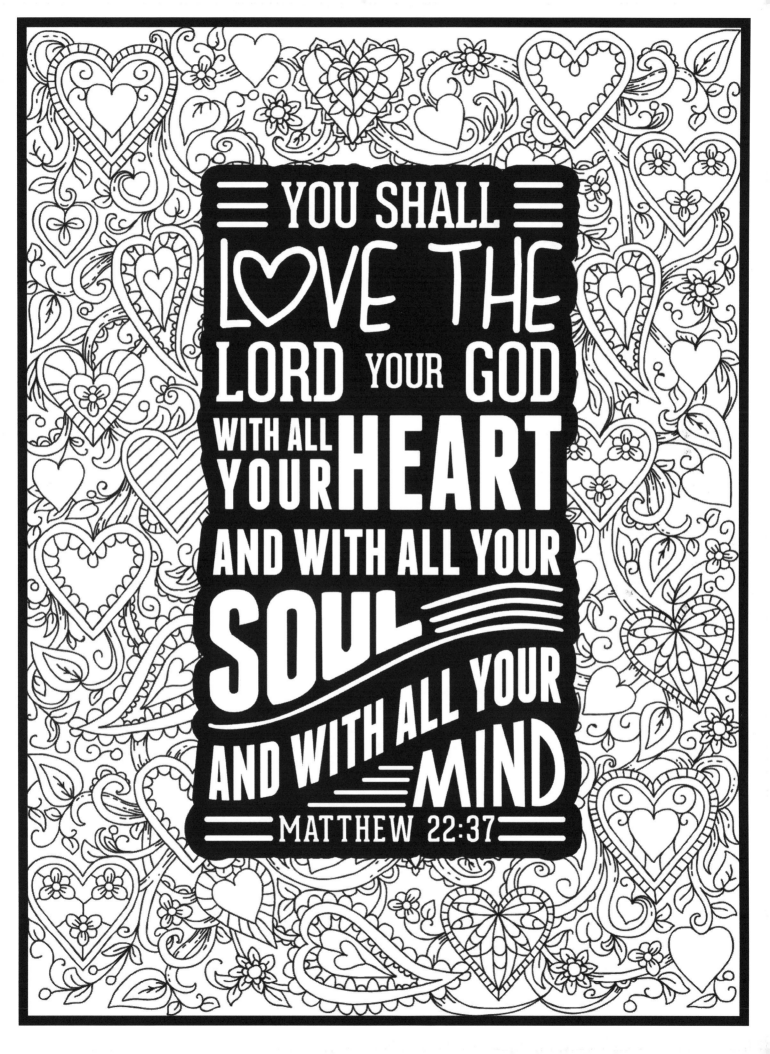

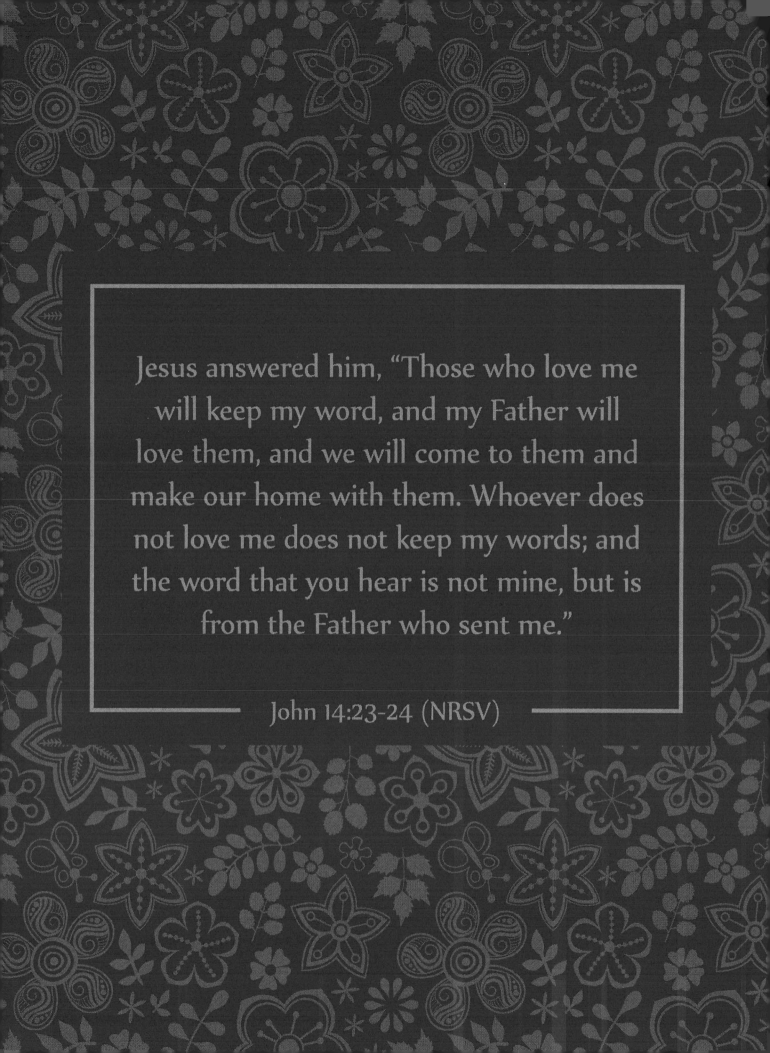

Jesus answered him, "Those who love me will keep my word, and my Father will love them, and we will come to them and make our home with them. Whoever does not love me does not keep my words; and the word that you hear is not mine, but is from the Father who sent me."

John 14:23-24 (NRSV)

those who love me will keep my word.

JOHN 14:23

"Be careful not to practice your righteousness in front of people, to be seen by them. Otherwise, you will have no reward from your Father in heaven. So whenever you give to the poor, don't sound a trumpet before you, as the hypocrites do in the synagogues and on the streets, to be applauded by people. I assure you: They've got their reward!"

Matthew 6:1-2 (HCSB)

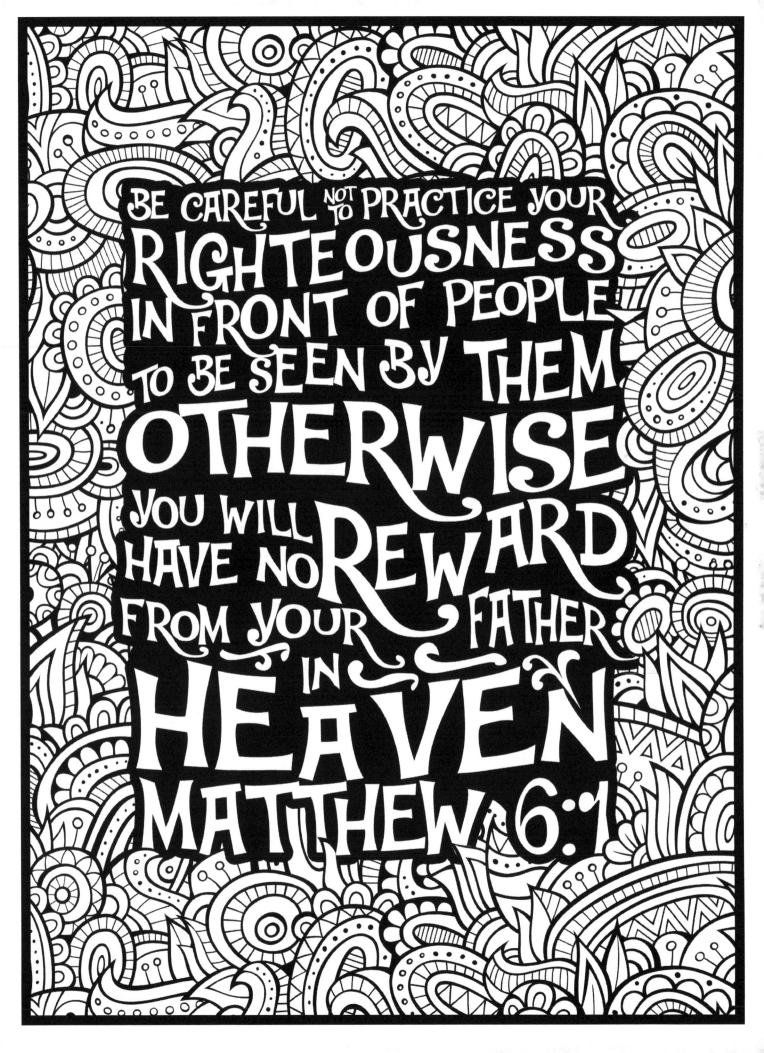

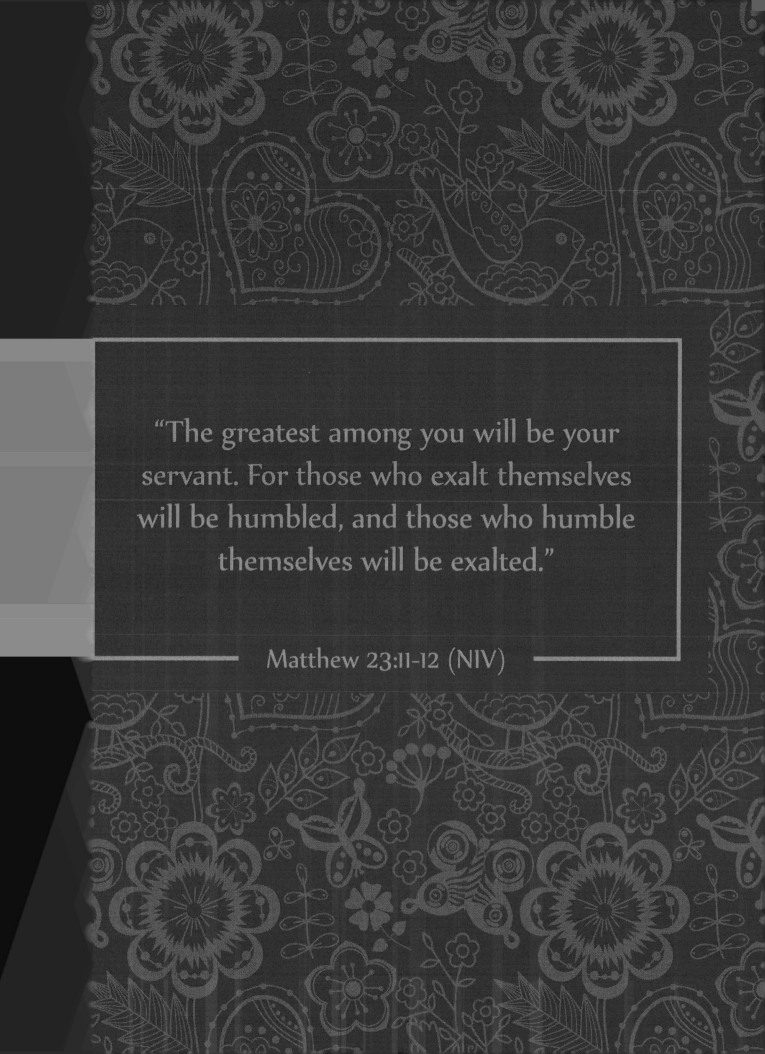

"The greatest among you will be your servant. For those who exalt themselves will be humbled, and those who humble themselves will be exalted."

Matthew 23:11-12 (NIV)

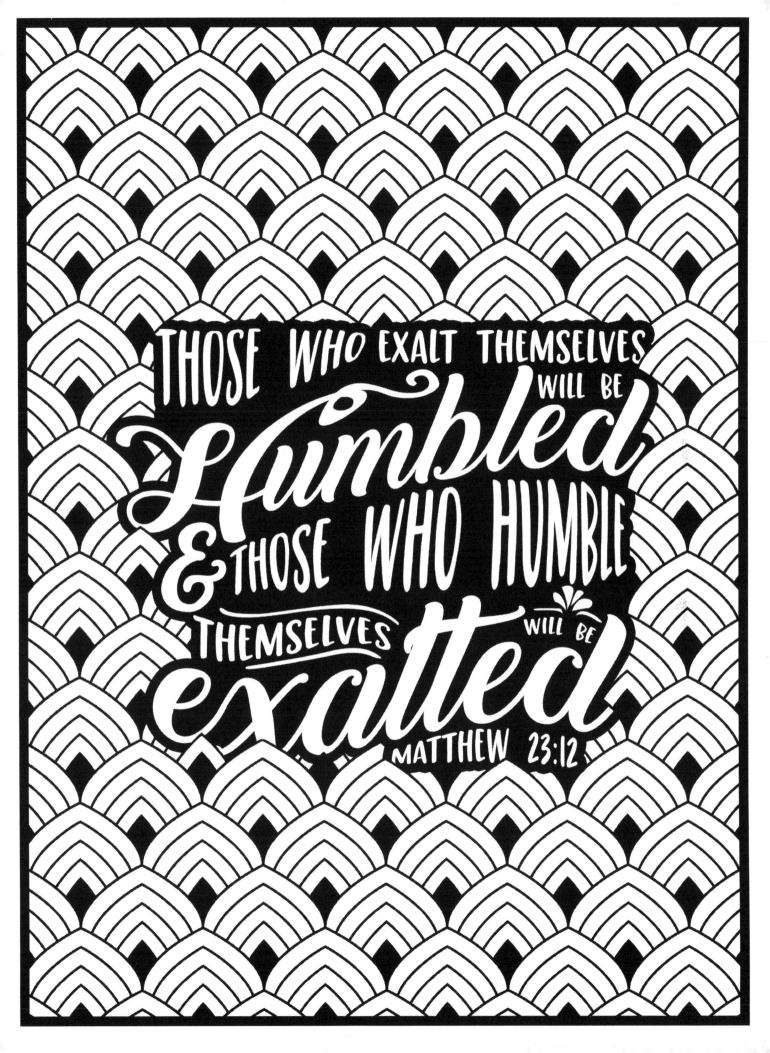

THOSE WHO EXALT THEMSELVES WILL BE Humbled & THOSE WHO HUMBLE THEMSELVES WILL BE exalted MATTHEW 23:12

And Jesus, walking by the Sea of Galilee, saw two brothers, Simon called Peter, and Andrew his brother, casting a net into the sea; for they were fishermen. Then he said to them, "Follow me, and I will make you fishers of men."

Matthew 4:18-19 (NKJV)

"You are the light of the world. A city built on a hill cannot be hid. No one after lighting a lamp puts it under the bushel basket, but on the lampstand, and it gives light to all in the house. In the same way, let your light shine before others, so that they may see your good works and give glory to your Father in heaven."

Matthew 5:14-16 (NRSV)

"So don't worry about these things, saying, 'What will we eat? What will we drink? What will we wear?' These things dominate the thoughts of unbelievers, but your heavenly Father already knows all your needs. Seek the Kingdom of God above all else, and live righteously, and he will give you everything you need. So don't worry about tomorrow, for tomorrow will bring its own worries. Today's trouble is enough for today."

Matthew 6:31-34 (NLT)

Seek the kingdom of GOD above all else and live righteously and he will give you EVERYTHING you need

~ MATTHEW 6:33 ~

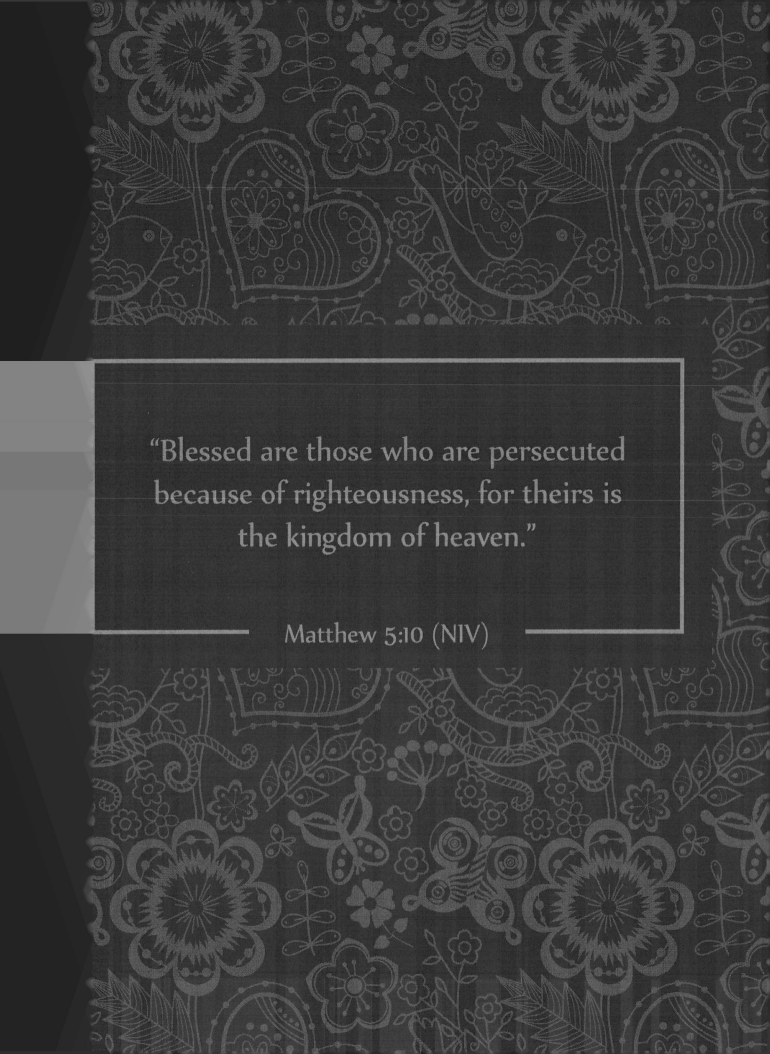

"Blessed are those who are persecuted because of righteousness, for theirs is the kingdom of heaven."

Matthew 5:10 (NIV)

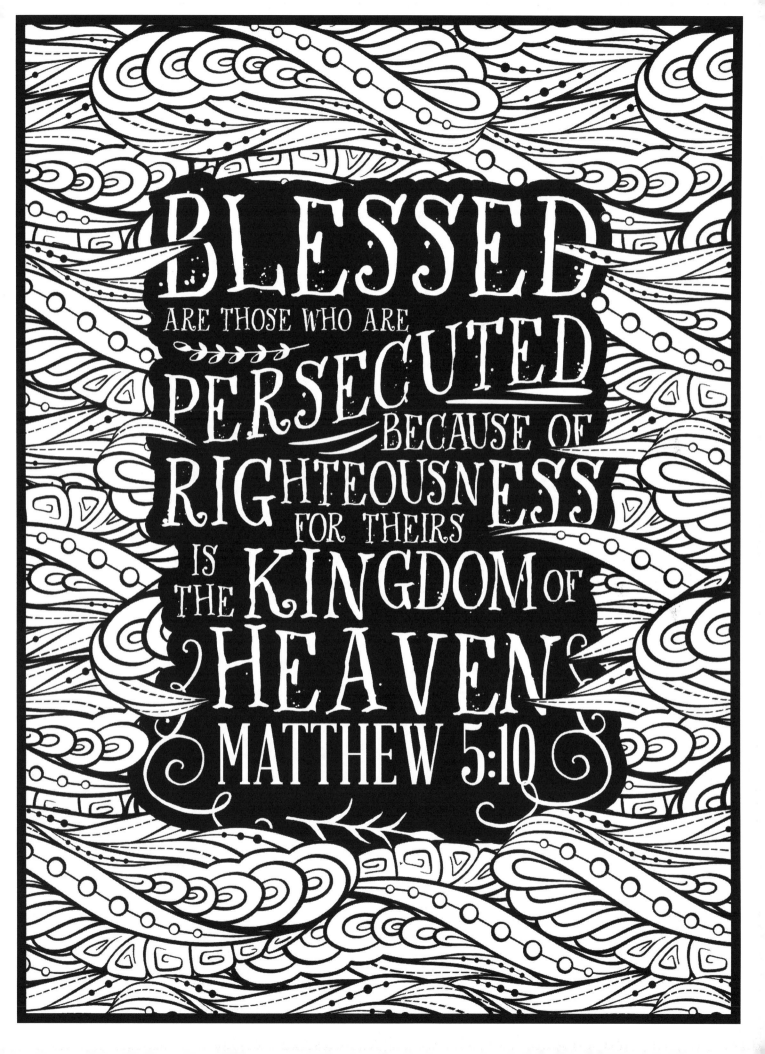

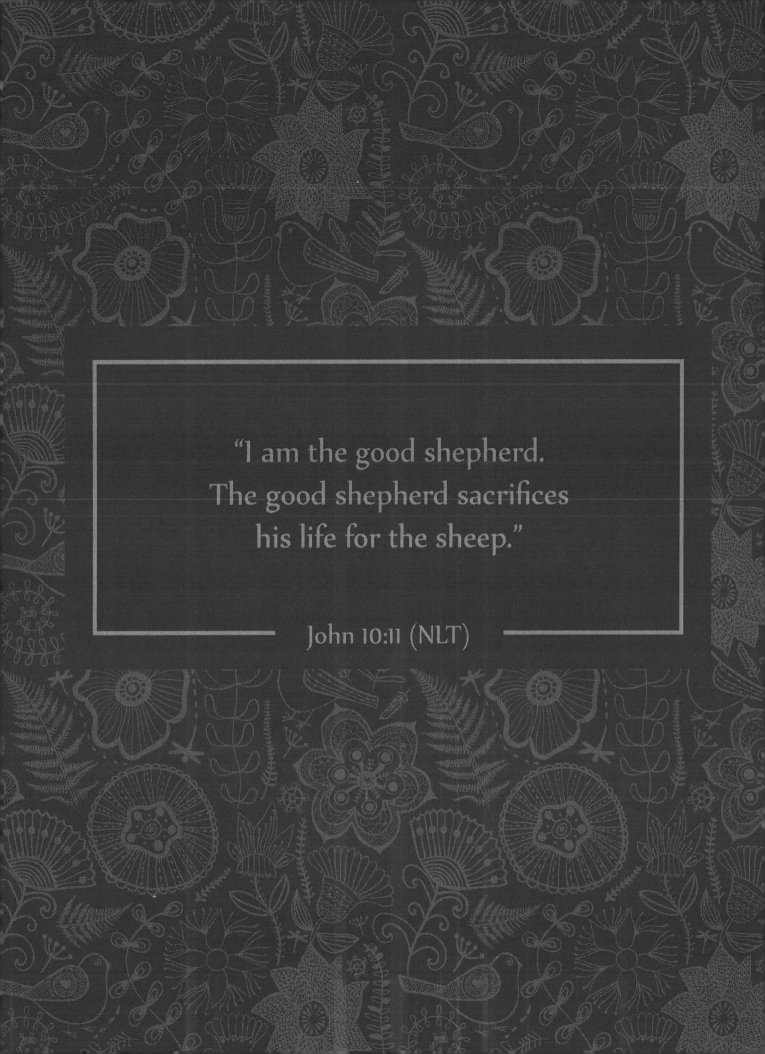

"I am the good shepherd.
The good shepherd sacrifices
his life for the sheep."

John 10:11 (NLT)

"For if you forgive others their trespasses, your heavenly Father will also forgive you; but if you do not forgive others, neither will your Father forgive your trespasses."

Matthew 6:14-15 (NRSV)

"Whenever you pray, you must not be like the hypocrites, because they love to pray standing in the synagogues and on the street corners to be seen by people. I assure you: They've got their reward! But when you pray, go into your private room, shut your door, and pray to your Father who is in secret. And your Father who sees in secret will reward you."

Matthew 6:5-6 (HCSB)

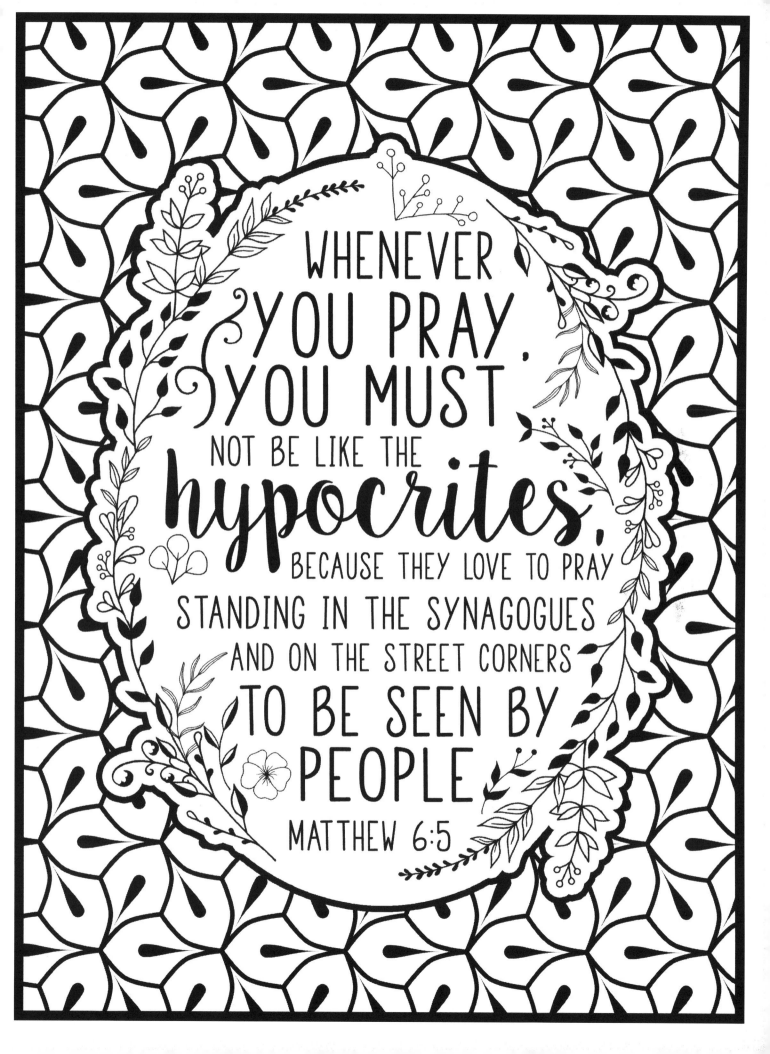

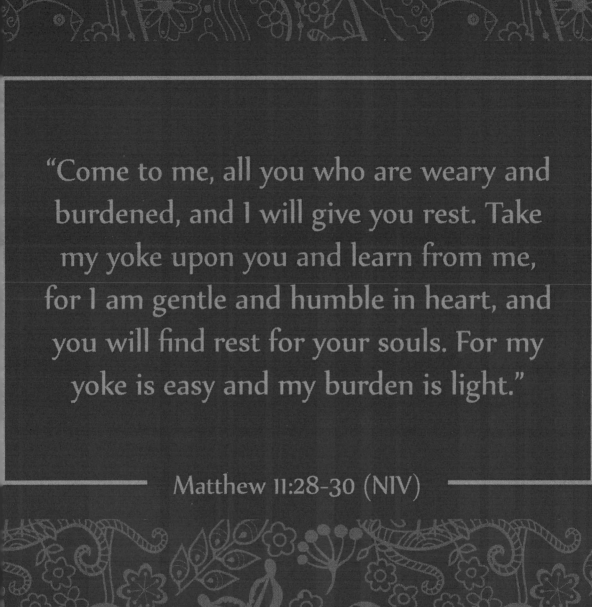

"Come to me, all you who are weary and burdened, and I will give you rest. Take my yoke upon you and learn from me, for I am gentle and humble in heart, and you will find rest for your souls. For my yoke is easy and my burden is light."

Matthew 11:28-30 (NIV)

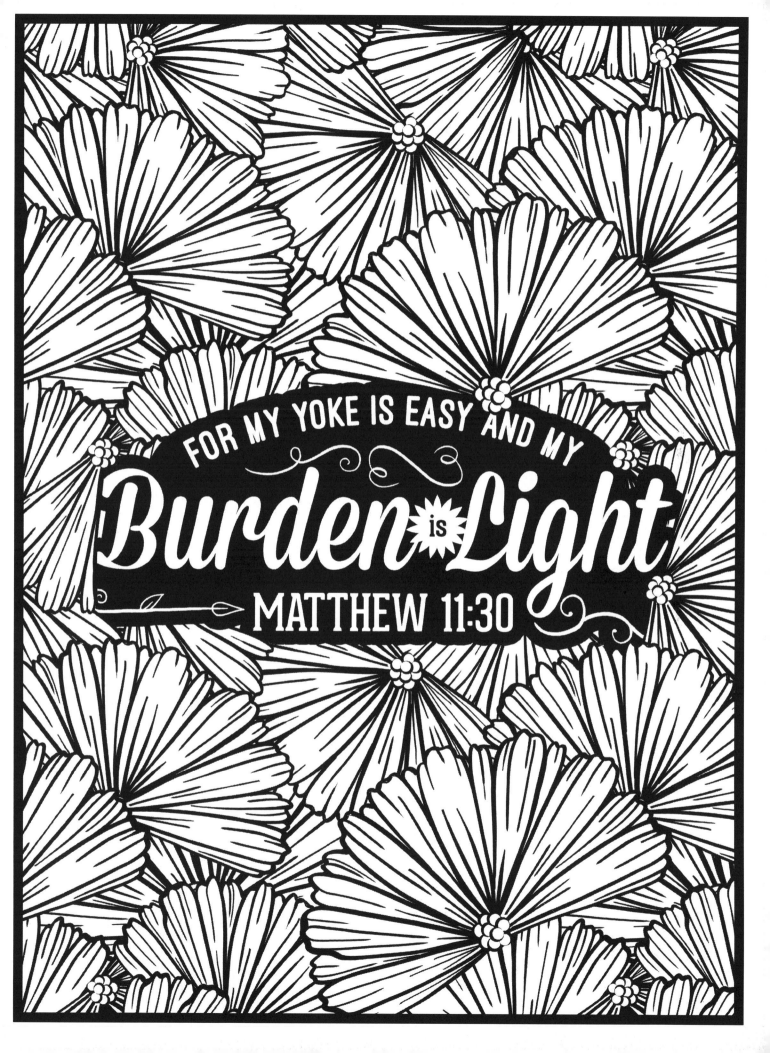

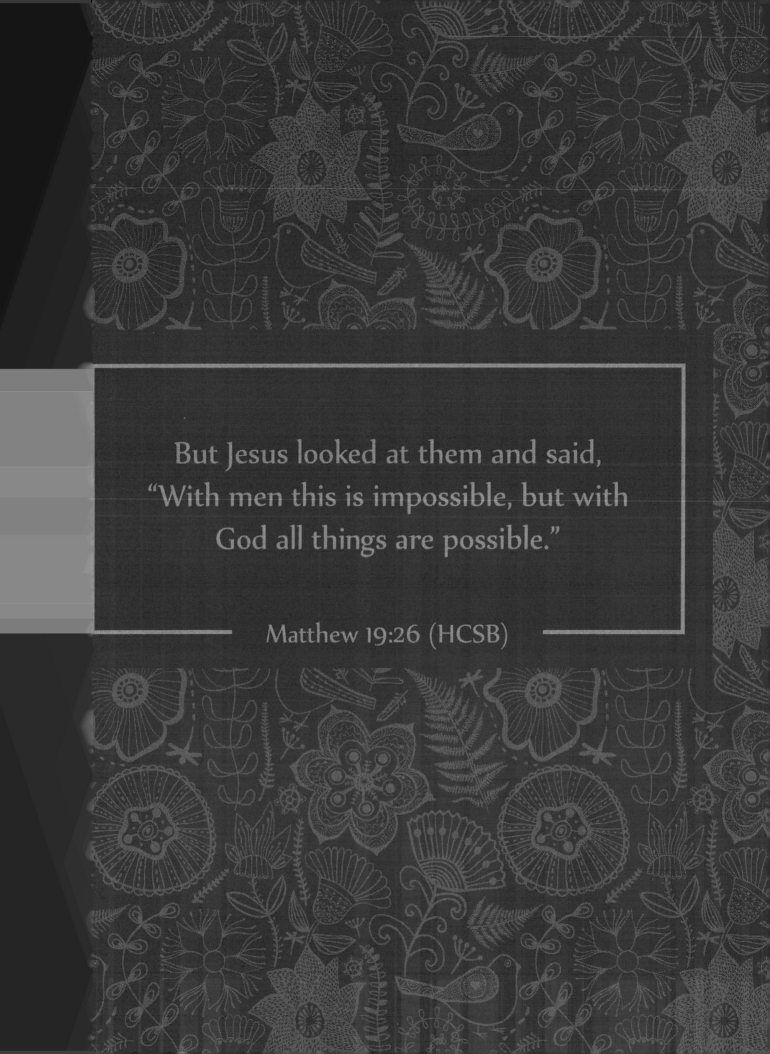

But Jesus looked at them and said, "With men this is impossible, but with God all things are possible."

Matthew 19:26 (HCSB)

Jesus answered and said to her, "Whoever drinks of this water will thirst again, but whoever drinks of the water that I shall give him will never thirst. But the water that I shall give him will become in him a fountain of water springing up into everlasting life."

John 4:13-14 (NKJV)

Jesus answered, "Those who are well have no need of a physician, but those who are sick; I have come to call not the righteous but sinners to repentance."

Luke 5:31-32 (NRSV)

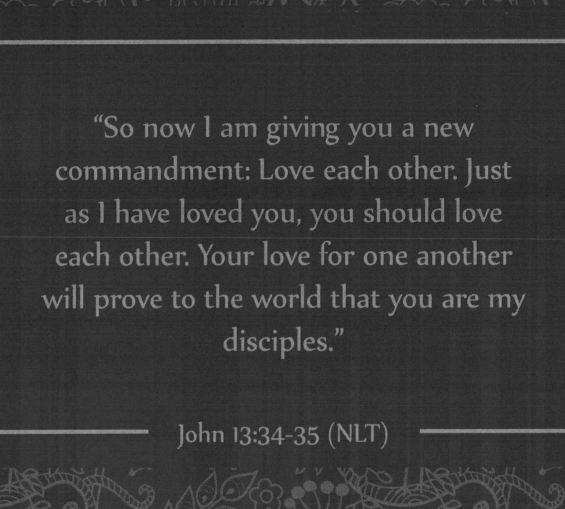

"So now I am giving you a new commandment: Love each other. Just as I have loved you, you should love each other. Your love for one another will prove to the world that you are my disciples."

John 13:34-35 (NLT)

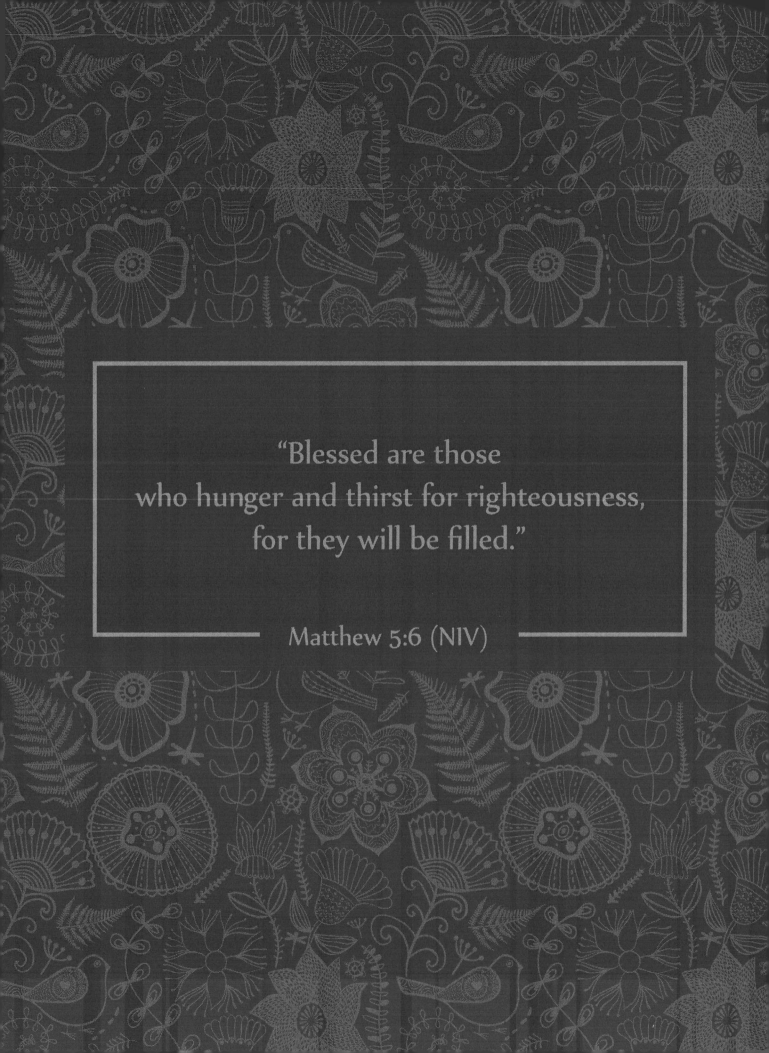

"Blessed are those
who hunger and thirst for righteousness,
for they will be filled."

Matthew 5:6 (NIV)

He said to them, "Go into the whole world and proclaim the gospel to every creature. Whoever believes and is baptized will be saved; whoever does not believe will be condemned."

Mark 16:15-16 (NABRE)

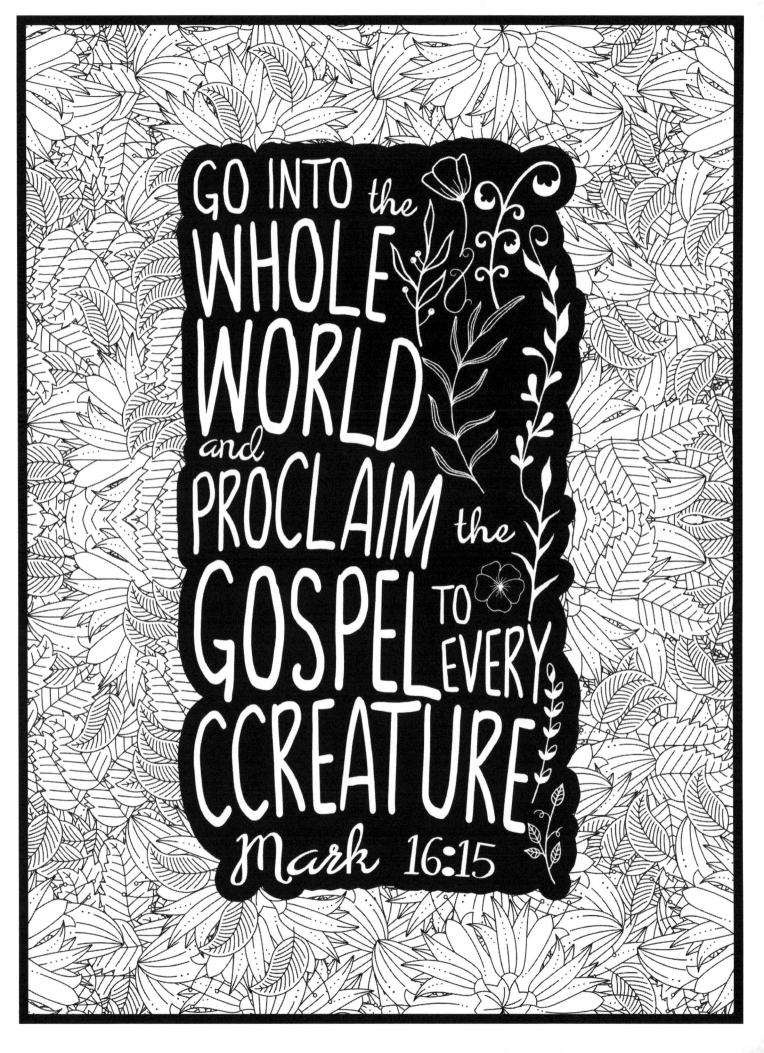

Jesus responded to them, "Do you now believe? Look: An hour is coming, and has come, when each of you will be scattered to his own home, and you will leave me alone. Yet I am not alone, because the Father is with me. I have told you these things so that in me you may have peace. You will have suffering in this world. Be courageous! I have conquered the world.

John 16:31-33 (HCSB)

"The time has come," he said.
"The kingdom of God has come near.
Repent and believe the good news!"

Mark 1:15 (NIV)

the
KINGDOM
of GOD
HAS COME NEAR
Repent
~and~
BELIEVE
The
Good
News!
MARK 1:15

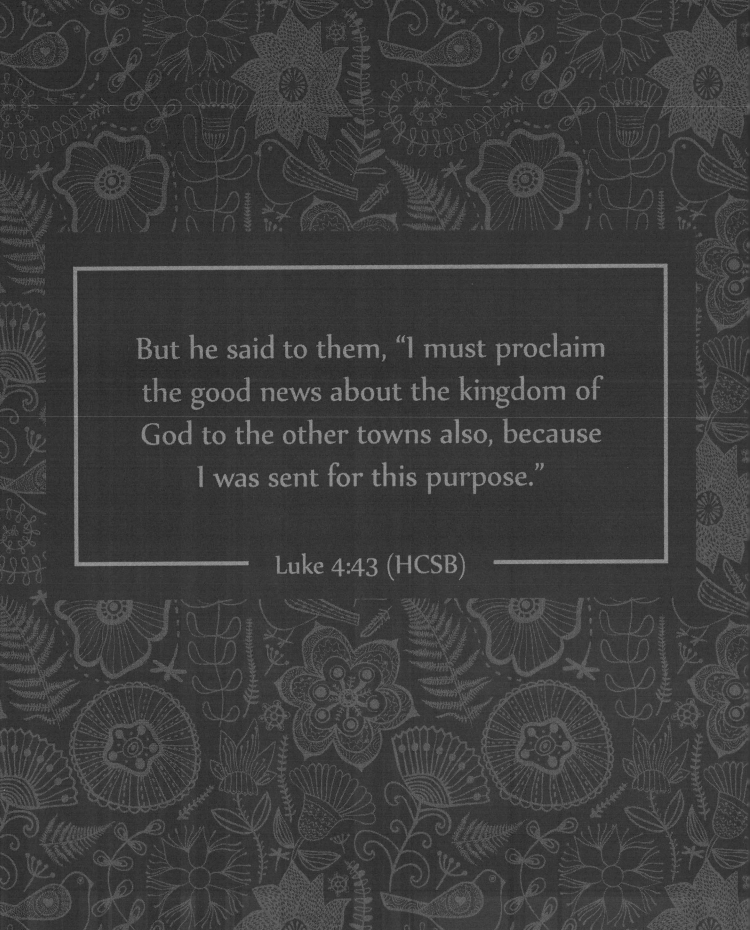

But he said to them, "I must proclaim the good news about the kingdom of God to the other towns also, because I was sent for this purpose."

Luke 4:43 (HCSB)

I MUST PROCLAIM THE GOOD NEWS ABOUT THE kingdom of God TO THE OTHER TOWNS ALSO, BECAUSE I WAS SENT FOR THIS PURPOSE

LUKE 4:43

Jesus answered, "Most assuredly, I say to you, unless one is born of water and the Spirit, he cannot enter the kingdom of God. That which is born of the flesh is flesh, and that which is born of the Spirit is spirit. Do not marvel that I said to you, 'You must be born again.'"

John 3:5-7 (NKJV)

UNLESS ONE IS Born OF Water and the Spirit HE Cannot ENTER THE KINGDOM OF GOD JOHN 3:5

To the Jews who had believed him, Jesus said, "If you hold to my teaching, you are really my disciples. Then you will know the truth, and the truth will set you free."

John 8:31-32 (NIV)

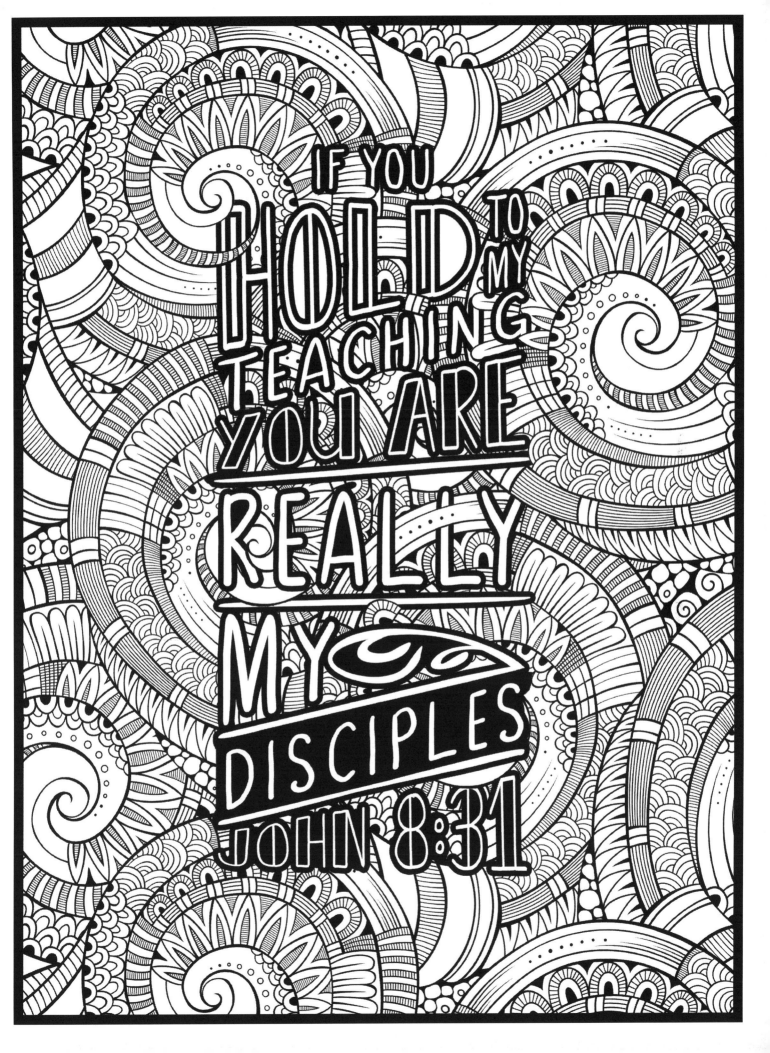

Then Jesus spoke to them again: "I am the light of the world. Anyone who follows me will never walk in the darkness but will have the light of life."

John 8:12 (HCSB)

Jesus said to them, "Very truly, I tell you, the Son can do nothing on his own, but only what he sees the Father doing; for whatever the Father does, the Son does likewise. The Father loves the Son and shows him all that he himself is doing; and he will show him greater works than these, so that you will be astonished."

John 5:19-20 (NRSV)

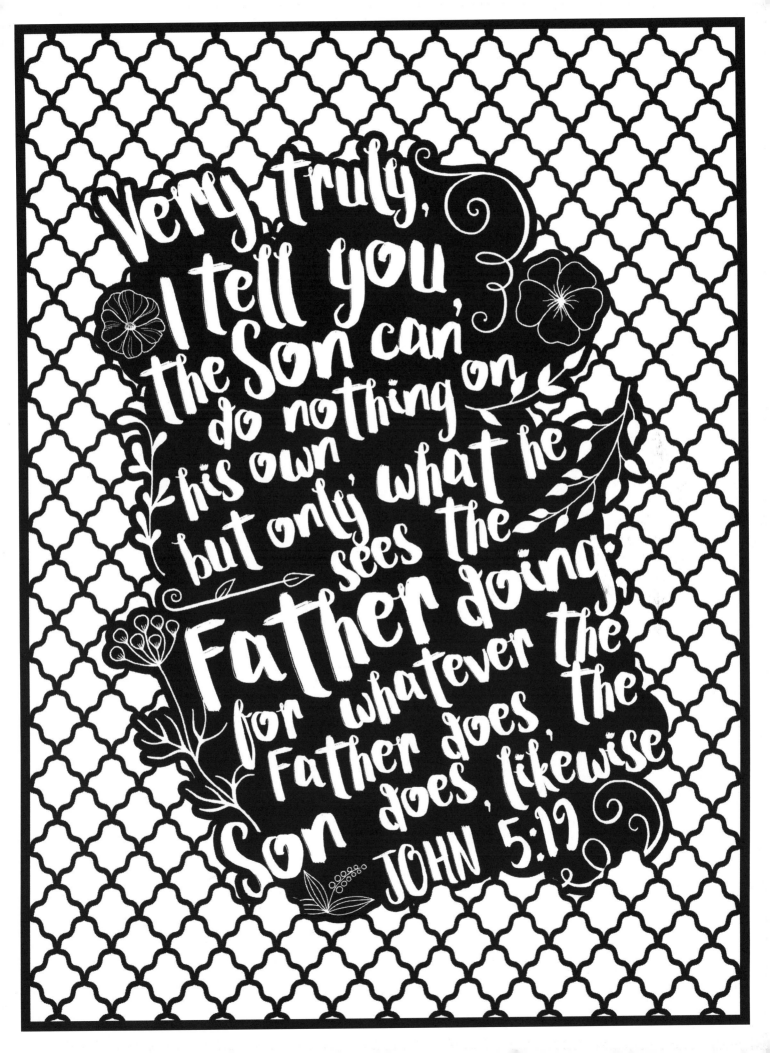

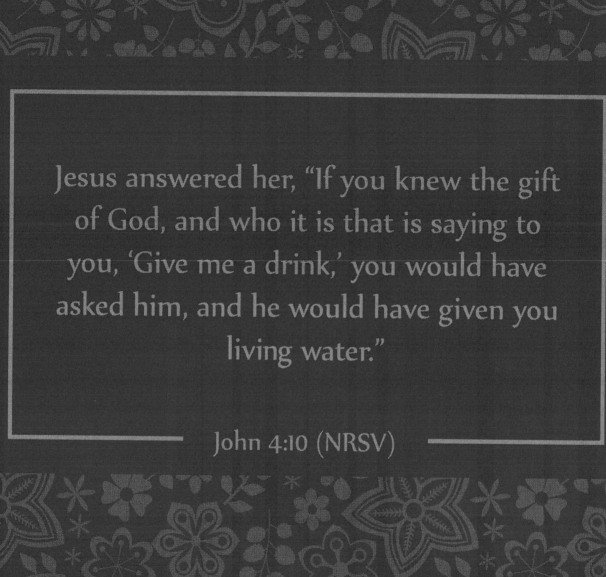

Jesus answered her, "If you knew the gift of God, and who it is that is saying to you, 'Give me a drink,' you would have asked him, and he would have given you living water."

John 4:10 (NRSV)

On the last day, that great day of the feast, Jesus stood and cried out, saying, "If anyone thirsts, let him come to me and drink. He who believes in me, as the Scripture has said, out of his heart will flow rivers of living water."

John 7:37-38 (NKJV)

Again he said, "Peace be with you.
As the Father has sent me,
so I am sending you."

John 20:21 (NLT)

When they came to the place called the Skull, they crucified him there, along with the criminals – one on his right, the other on his left. Jesus said, "Father, forgive them, for they do not know what they are doing." And they divided up his clothes by casting lots.

Luke 23:33-34 (NIV)

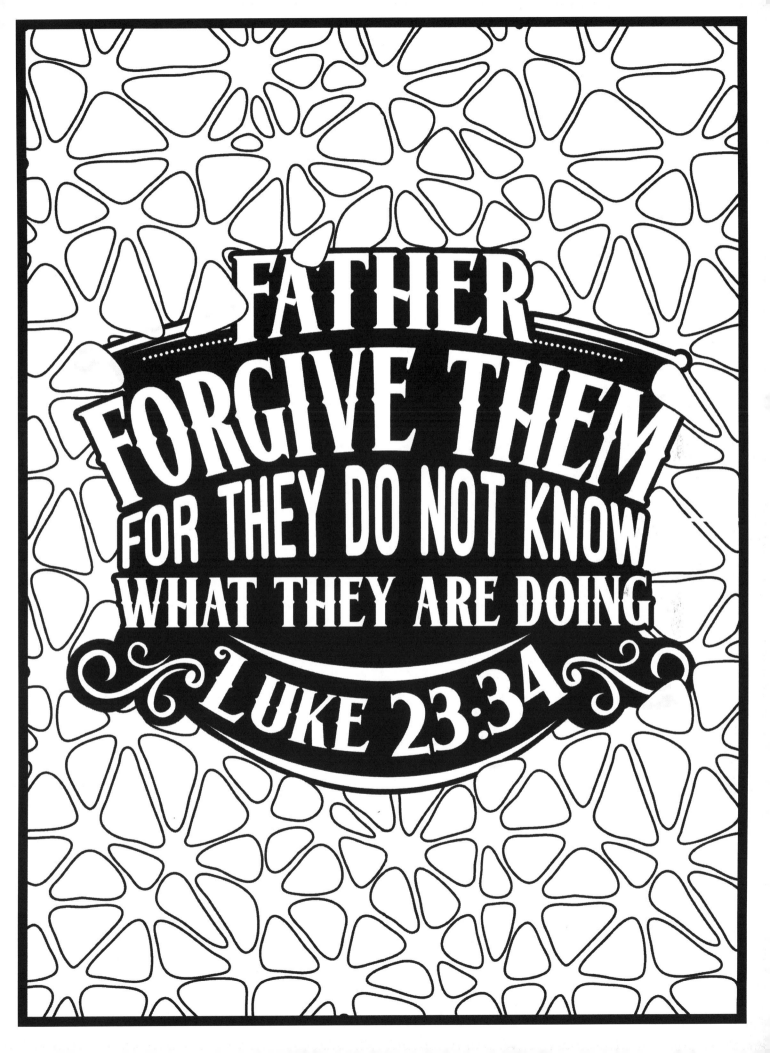

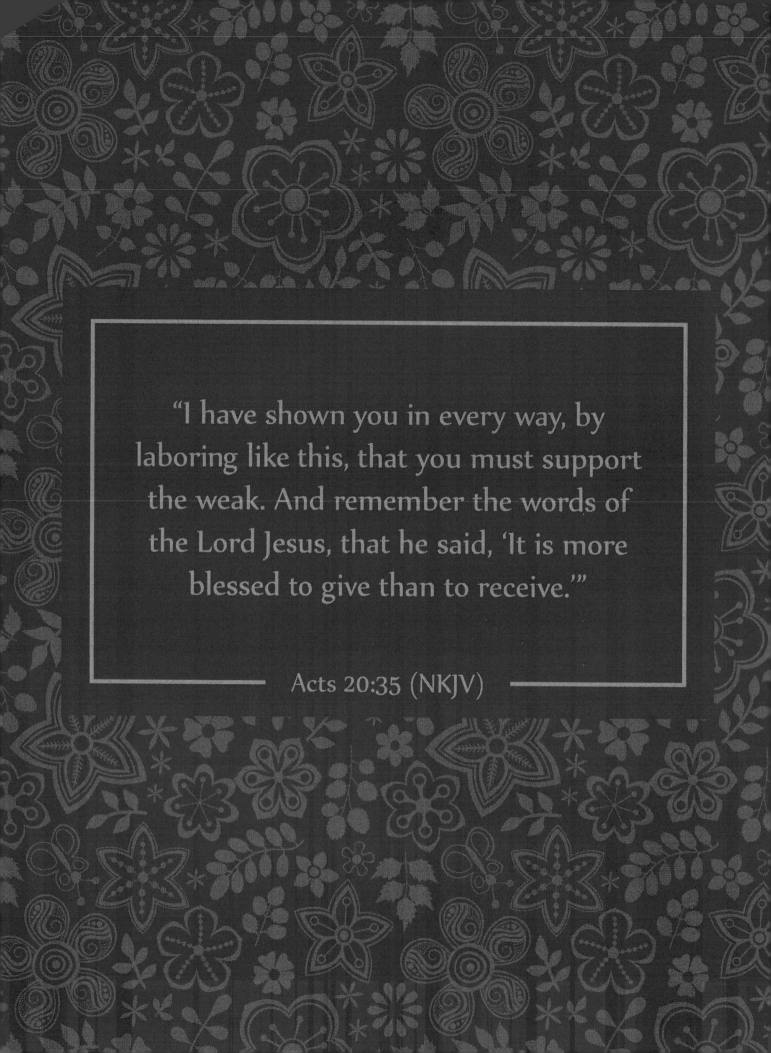

"I have shown you in every way, by laboring like this, that you must support the weak. And remember the words of the Lord Jesus, that he said, 'It is more blessed to give than to receive.'"

Acts 20:35 (NKJV)

Then Jesus said to him,
"'If You can'? Everything is possible
to the one who believes."

Mark 9:23 (HCSB)

"I am the true vine, and my Father is the vinegrower. He removes every branch in me that bears no fruit. Every branch that bears fruit he prunes to make it bear more fruit. You have already been cleansed by the word that I have spoken to you. Abide in me as I abide in you. Just as the branch cannot bear fruit by itself unless it abides in the vine, neither can you unless you abide in me."

John 15:1-4 (NRSV)

"This is my commandment: love one another as I love you. No one has greater love than this, to lay down one's life for one's friends. You are my friends if you do what I command you. I no longer call you slaves, because a slave does not know what his master is doing. I have called you friends, because I have told you everything I have heard from my Father."

John 15:12–15 (NABRE)

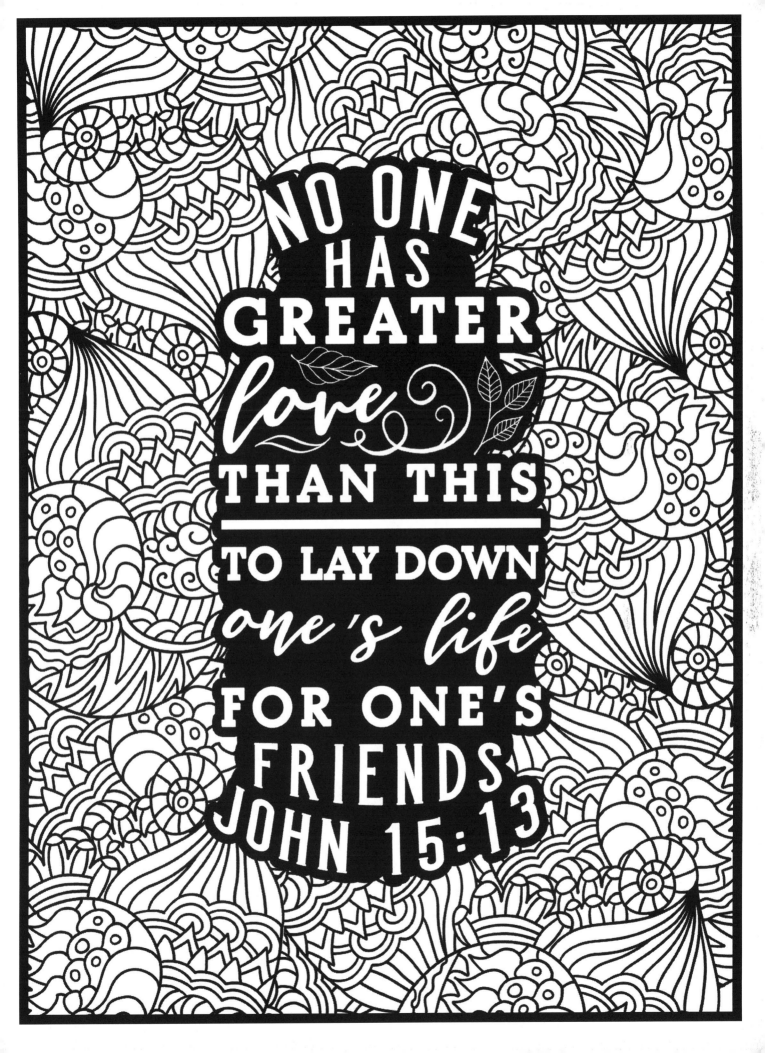

"If the world hates you, realize that it hated me first. If you belonged to the world, the world would love its own; but because you do not belong to the world, and I have chosen you out of the world, the world hates you."

John 15:18-19 (NABRE)

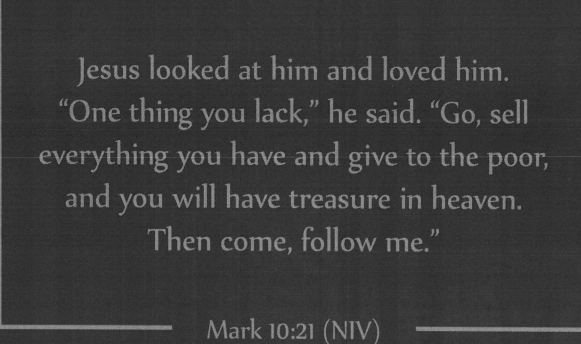

Jesus looked at him and loved him. "One thing you lack," he said. "Go, sell everything you have and give to the poor, and you will have treasure in heaven. Then come, follow me."

Mark 10:21 (NIV)

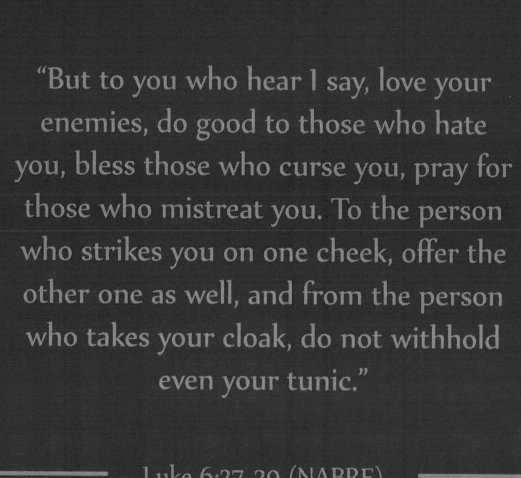

"But to you who hear I say, love your enemies, do good to those who hate you, bless those who curse you, pray for those who mistreat you. To the person who strikes you on one cheek, offer the other one as well, and from the person who takes your cloak, do not withhold even your tunic."

Luke 6:27-29 (NABRE)

"Stop judging and you will not be judged. Stop condemning and you will not be condemned. Forgive and you will be forgiven. Give and gifts will be given to you; a good measure, packed together, shaken down, and overflowing, will be poured into your lap. For the measure with which you measure will in return be measured out to you."

Luke 6:37-38 (NABRE)

Then he said to all, "If anyone wishes to come after me, he must deny himself and take up his cross daily and follow me. For whoever wishes to save his life will lose it, but whoever loses his life for my sake will save it."

Luke 9:23-24 (NABRE)

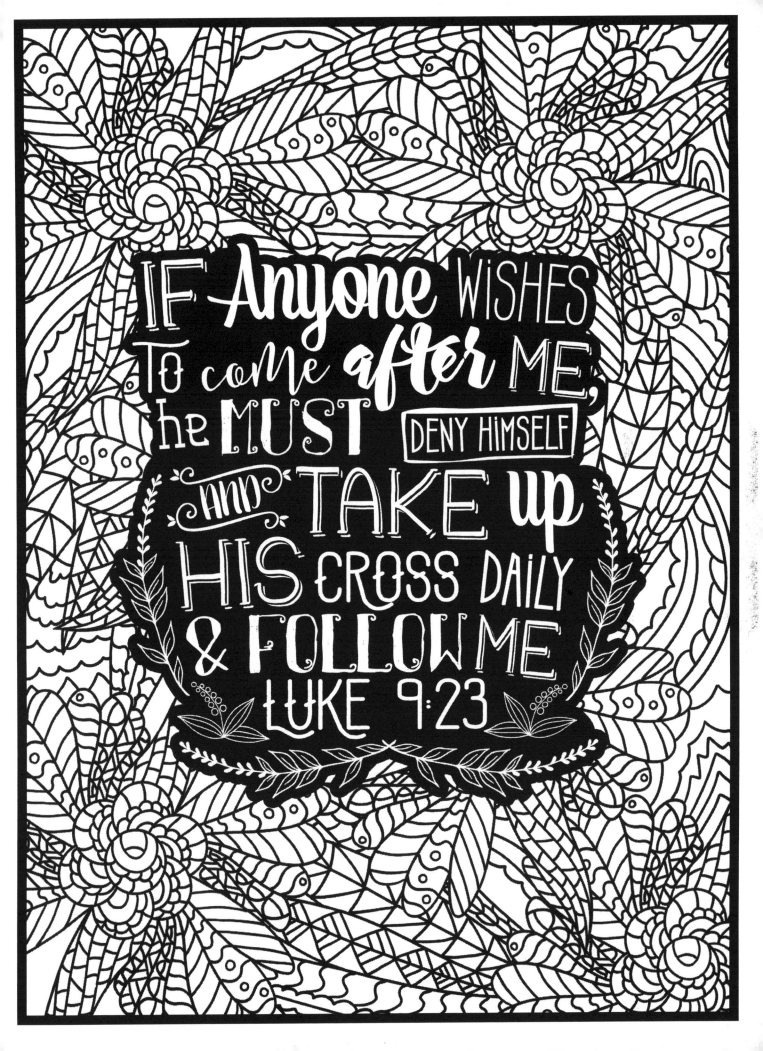

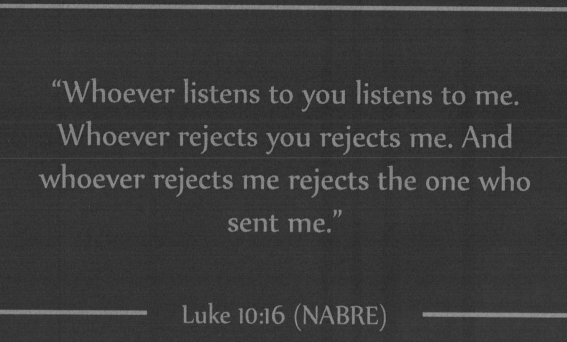

"Whoever listens to you listens to me. Whoever rejects you rejects me. And whoever rejects me rejects the one who sent me."

Luke 10:16 (NABRE)

He said to them, "When you pray, say:

"'Father, hallowed be your name, your kingdom come. Give us each day our daily bread. Forgive us our sins, for we also forgive everyone who sins against us. And lead us not into temptation.'"

Luke 11:2-4 (NIV)

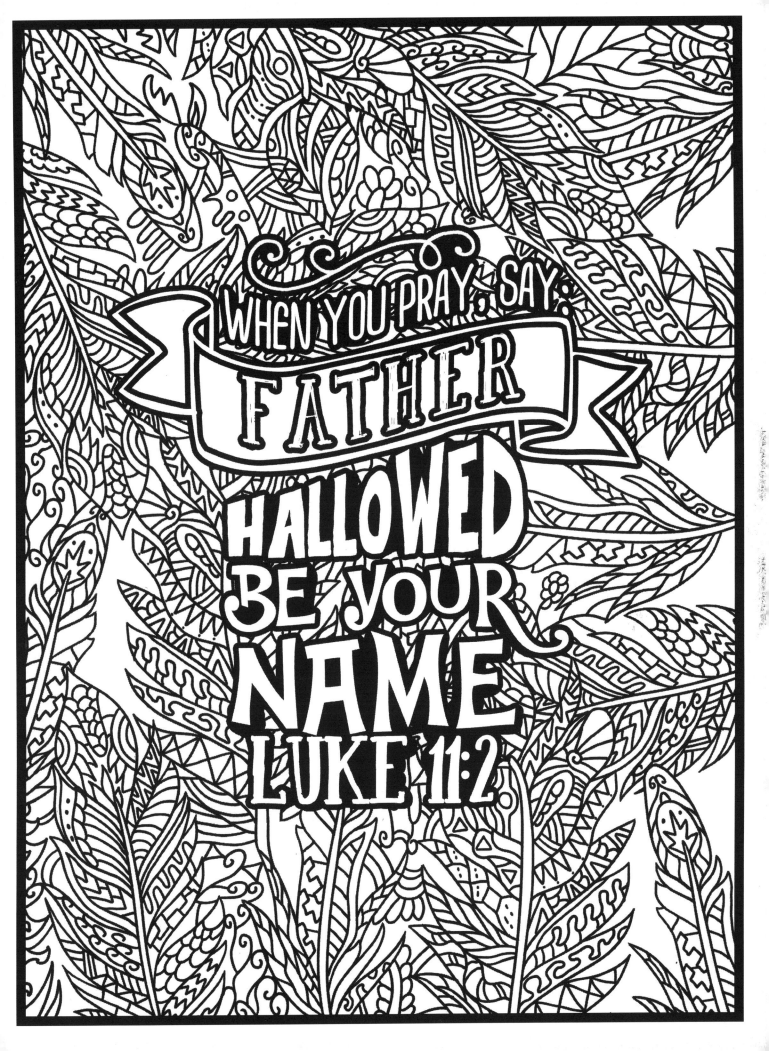

When Jesus saw this he became indignant and said to them, "Let the children come to me; do not prevent them, for the kingdom of God belongs to such as these. Amen, I say to you, whoever does not accept the kingdom of God like a child will not enter it."

Mark 10:14-15 (NABRE)

"Amen, I say to you, whoever says to this mountain, 'Be lifted up and thrown into the sea,' and does not doubt in his heart but believes that what he says will happen, it shall be done for him. Therefore I tell you, all that you ask for in prayer, believe that you will receive it and it shall be yours. When you stand to pray, forgive anyone against whom you have a grievance, so that your heavenly Father may in turn forgive you your transgressions."

Mark 11:23-25 (NABRE)

BE SURE TO FOLLOW US
ON SOCIAL MEDIA
FOR THE LATEST NEWS,
SNEAK PEEKS, & GIVEAWAYS

inspiredtograce

Inspired-to-Grace

@inspired2grace

ADD YOURSELF TO OUR
MONTHLY NEWSLETTER FOR FREE DIGITAL
DOWNLOADS AND DISCOUNT CODES
www.inspiredtograce.com/newsletter

CHECK OUT OUR OTHER BOOKS!

WWW.INSPIREDTOGRACE.COM

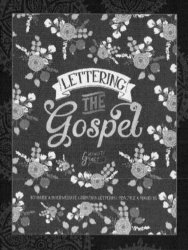 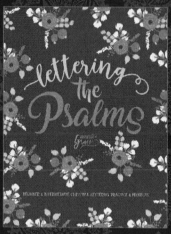  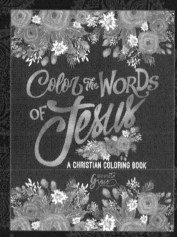

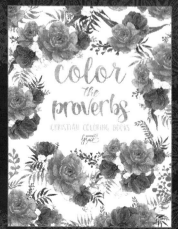 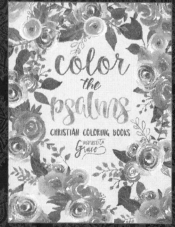

CHECK OUT OUR OTHER BOOKS!

WWW.INSPIREDTOGRACE.COM

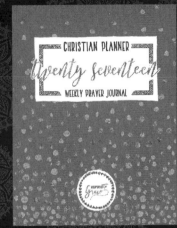
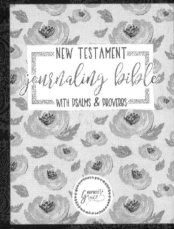

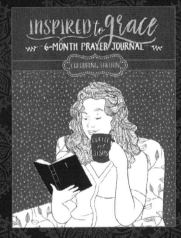

CHECK OUT OUR OTHER BOOKS!

WWW.INSPIREDTOGRACE.COM

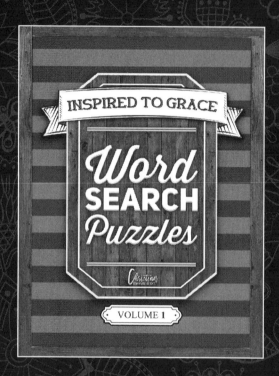

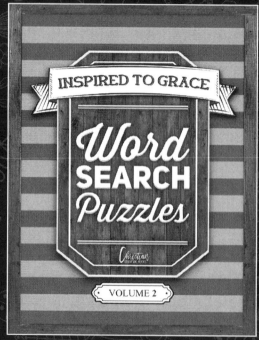

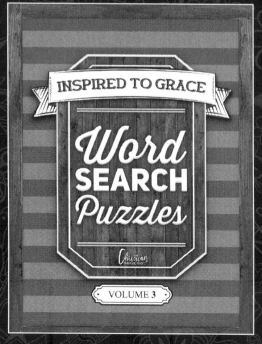

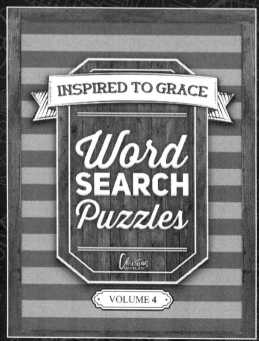

32998274R00055

Printed in Great Britain
by Amazon